Reflections of Puerto Penasco

My thoughts and memories of the sea

Books With Soul

For Iris, Ashley & Jill who love Rocky Point

Books With Soul
Somewhere in the desert, sea and forest.
www.bookswithsoul.com
∞

First Edition 2018

Printed in the United States of America

ISBN-13 978-1-949325-31-7

This book belongs to:

____

I started collecting my memories of Puerto Penasco (Rocky Point) on this day:

____

life is a collection of moments

-unknown

The sea lives in every one of us.- *Wyland*

Whether you purchased this journal for yourself or received it as a gift. YOU are special.

Some may even call you LUCKY.
You're smart.
You're wise.
And, you love the sea.

Someday, you will have a collection of your memories.

Moments and thoughts that occurred in your life. Moments you took the time to write down in this book.

You are *A Collector of Memories.*
So, whether it is your first visit to the sea, or one of many, you will have a collection of your thoughts and memories.

Write a note down every day, sit by the water and write a poem, or sketch a picture in the blank pages.

Perhaps, you want to write down all the different restaurants you visited while on vacation and assign them your own special rating.

Or perhaps, a quick paragraph of where you stayed, who you traveled with and a funny moment.

Maybe the sea speaks to you and inspires you to write a story.

This is your journal, use it as you like.

But please use it. Let it get sandy, worn and used. Fill it's pages with memories.
Your memories.
Your Words. Your Pages.

Puerto Penasco aka Rocky Point

Doodle, scribble, print, draw,

it's up to you.

Write in the lines, color

outside the lines, write upside

down.

You decide...

Ideas on what to write each
day?
Anything, nothing, everything:
a name,
a moment,
the weather,
a historical event,
a unique moment,
the birth of a child,
the death of a friend,
the love of your heart,
a reflection of time,
a crazy fun night,
adventures with friends,
a few words to describe your
mood.
Anything, nothing, everything.

It's your reflections.

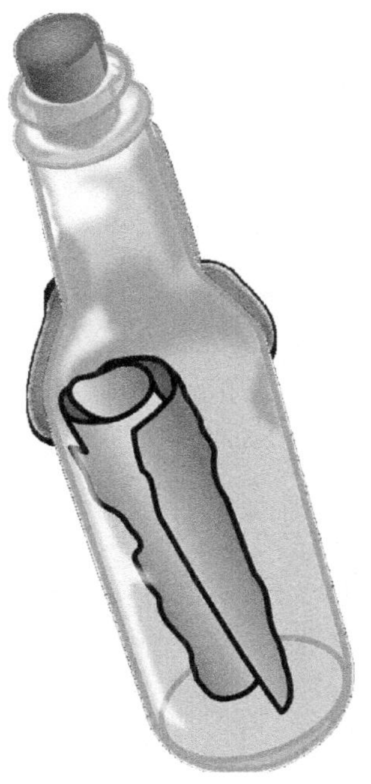

Today's date is:

____

What message would you write in a bottle?

____

____

____

____

____

____

____

Today's date is:

____

I want to remember this about Rocky Point:

____

____

____

____

____

____

____

____

____

Or if you don't want to write you can sketch a memory:

When I want to be free, I go to the sea,

that is where I find freedom.

A.K. Smith

Or if you don't want to write you can sketch a memory:

Today's date is:

____

I want to remember this about the weather:

Or if you don't want to write you can sketch a memory.

Life is too short not to have a little sand in your suitcase. Anita Kaltenbaugh

Or if you don't want to write you can sketch a memory.

Today's date is: ______________________________

I want to remember this about Mexico:

____

____

____

____

____

____

____

____

____

____

____

____

____

Or if you don't want to write you can sketch a memory.

In one drop of water are found all the secrets of all the oceans.

Kahill Gibran

Or if you don't want to write you can sketch a memory.

Today's date is: ______________________________

I want to remember this about today:

____

____

____

____

____

____

____

____

____

____

____

sketch a memory:

To me the sea is like a childhood friend, a person, I've known since I was 14. That is the first time I met the ocean. And, it has been a fabulous relationship.

-Anita Kaltenbaugh

Today's date is: ____________________________

I want to remember this about my vacation:

____

____

____

____

____

____

____

____

____

____

____

Set the alarm, wake up early in the morning and walk the beach.
What a fantastic way to start the day.
Viva Mexico.

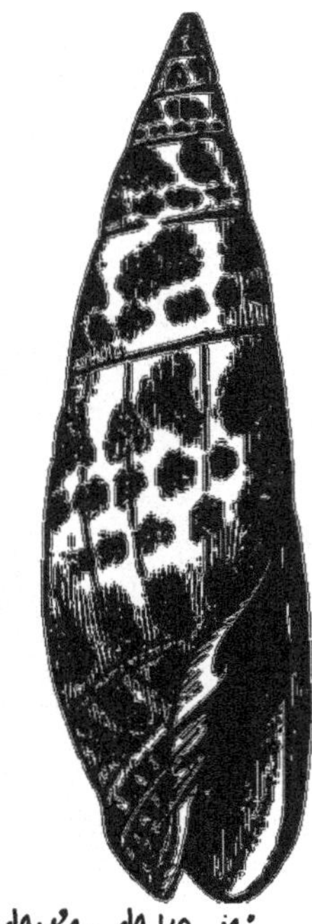

Today's date is:

____

I want to remember this:

To me the sea is a continual miracle;
The fishes that swim- the rocks- the
motion of the waves- the ships, with
men in them. What stranger miracles
are there?

-Walt Whitman

sketch a memory.

Today's date is:

I there is one thing about this day:

For whatever we lose (like a you or a me), it's always our self we find in the sea. – e e cummings

Today's date is:

____

I want to remember this about the ocean:

____

____

____

____

____

____

____

____

____

____

____

Fishes live in the sea, as men do a-land;

the great ones eat up the little ones.

William Shakespeare

Today's date is:

____

I want to remember this:

____

____

____

____

____

____

____

____

sketch a memory.

The sweetest shrimp in all the world is

in Rocky Point, Mexico.

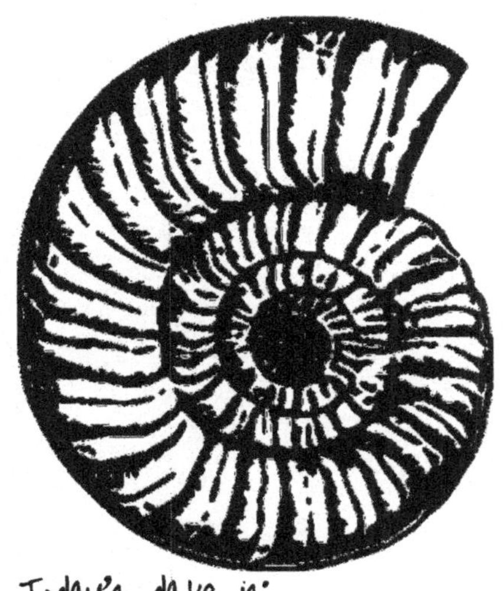

Today's date is:

____

I want to remember this about the world:

____

____

____

____

____

____

____

____

____

____

____

The sea! the sea! the open sea! The blue, the fresh, the ever free!

Bryan W. Procter

Today's date is:

____

I want to remember this about ocean:

____

____

____

____

____

____

____

____

____

____

Eternity begins and ends with the ocean's tides. - *Unknown*

sketch a memory.

Today's date is:

____

I want to remember this event:

Limitless and immortal, the waters are the beginning and end of all things on earth. Heinrich Zimmer

Today's date is:

____

I want to remember this about Mexico:

____

____

____

____

____

____

____

____

____

____

____

____

____

____

You can never cross the ocean until you have the courage to lose sight of the shore. Christopher Columbus

Today's date is:

____

I want to remember this about today:

____

____

____

____

____

____

____

____

____

____

sketch a memory:

An empty beach, a setting sun, now I can relax in perfect solitude. A.K. Smith

Today's date is:

____

I want to remember my favorite foods in Rocky Point:

The Sea, once it casts its spell, holds one in its net of wonder forever.

Jacques Cousteau.

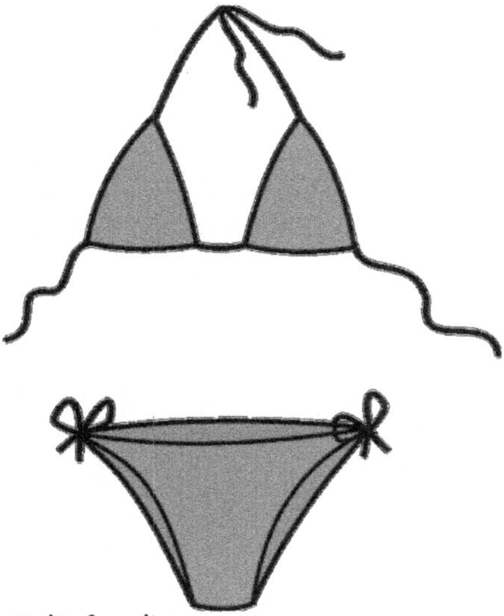

Today's date is:

____

I want to remember this about the ocean:

____

____

____

____

____

____

____

____

____

____

____

I could never stay long enough on the shore; the tang of the untainted fresh, and free sea air was like a cool, quieting thought. Helen Keller

sketch a memory:

Today's date is:

I want to remember this about today:

That the sea is one of the most beautiful and magnificent sights in Nature, all admit. John Joly

Today's date is:

____

I want to remember this about the world:

Old age: the estuary that enlarges and spreads itself grandly as it pours into the Great Sea. Walt Whitman

Today's date is:

____

A day at the beach I want to remember:

____

____

____

____

____

____

____

____

____

____

____

____

____

____

____

sketch a memory.

We ourselves feel that what we are doing is just a drop in the ocean. But the ocean would be less because of that missing drop. Mother Teresa

Today's date is:

____

I want to remember this about friends:

Our memories of the ocean will linger on, long after our foot prints in the sand are gone. anonymous

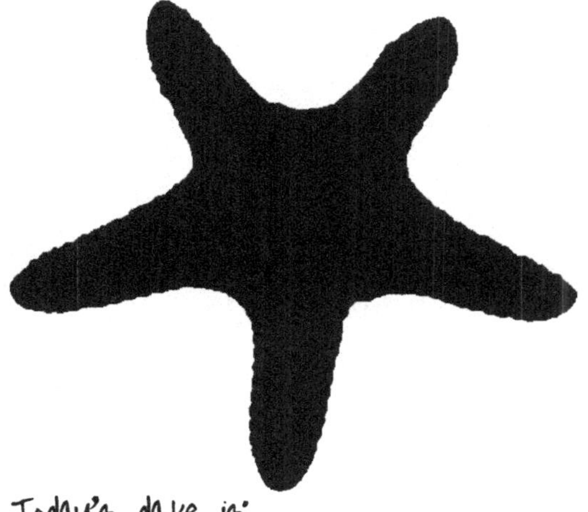

Today's date is:

____

I want to remember this about the ocean:

____

____

____

____

____

____

____

____

____

____

____

____

____

The pounding of the waves of the sea, is the best sleep machine invented. A.K. Smith

sketch a memory:

Today's date is:

I want to remember this about the sun:

The ocean kisses the sand, retreats and comes back again and again. A.K. Smith

Today's date is:

____

I want to remember this about love:

Writers begin with a grain of sand, and then create a beach. Robert Black

Today's date is:

____

I want to remember this about today:

sketch a memory:

To hell with luck, I'll bring the luck to me. Hemingway

Today's date is:

____

Living the beach life is great, I want to remember:

____

____

____

____

____

____

____

____

____

____

____

____

____

I love you and me by the sea.

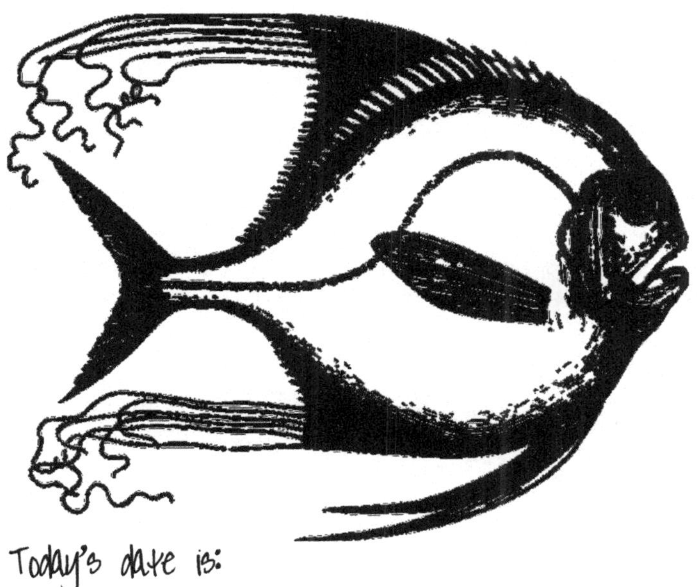

Today's date is:

____

I want to remember this about the ocean:

____

____

____

____

____

____

____

____

____

____

Bare feet and salty hair, seriously the best.

sketch a memory:

Today's date is:

____

I want to remember this about sandcastles:

I think it's time for a trip to the beach...my beach: Puerto Penasco

Today's date is:

____

I want to remember this about today:

Life is simple when you add water.

Today's date is:

____

I want to remember this favorite beach recipe:

sketch a memory:

I met the beach and fell in love. –

A.K. Smith

Today's date is:

____

I want to remember this about the ocean:

____

____

____

____

____

____

____

____

____

____

____

Why is it that you can smell the sea air and it's unlike any other air?

Today's date is:

I want to remember this about the sea life:

B.E.A.C.H. Best Escape Anyone Can Have. -Unknown

sketch a memory:

Today's date is:

____

I want to remember this about the day at the Malecon:

____

____

____

____

____

____

____

____

____

Is there a beach in heaven?

Today's date is:

____

I want to remember this about children at the beach:

____

____

____

____

____

____

____

____

____

____

____

____

____

The good seaman weathers the storm he cannot avoid, and avoids the storm he cannot weather. unknown

Today's date is:

I want to remember this moment of celebration:

sketch a memory.

I love the smell of the sea.

Today's date is:

____

I want to remember this about Puerto Penasco history:

____

____

____

____

____

____

____

____

____

____

____

____

____

Twenty years from now you will be more disappointed by the things that you didn't do than by the ones you did do. So throw off the bowlines. Sail away from the sage harbor. Catch the trade winds in your sails. Explore! Dream! Discover! Mark Twain

Today's date is:

____

I want to remember this about family:

____

____

____

____

____

____

____

____

____

____

____

He who loves practice without theory is like the sailor who boards ship without a rudder and compass and never knows where he may cast. -Leonardo da Vinci

sketch a memory.

Today's date is:

____

I want to remember this about the ocean:

Learn from yesterday, live for today, hope for tomorrow. The important thing is not to stop questioning.

-Albert Einstein

Today's date is:

____

I want to remember this about today:

____

____

____

____

____

____

____

____

____

____

____

____

____

Live in the sunshine, swim the sea,

drink the wild air.

Ralph Waldo Emerson

Today's date is:

____

I want to remember this about her:

sketch a memory:

Dear Ocean, thank you for making me realize how big I really am.

Today's date is:

____

I want to remember this about the sky:

The sea is comforting, the sun is warm and I just want to be close to the sea, as often as I can.

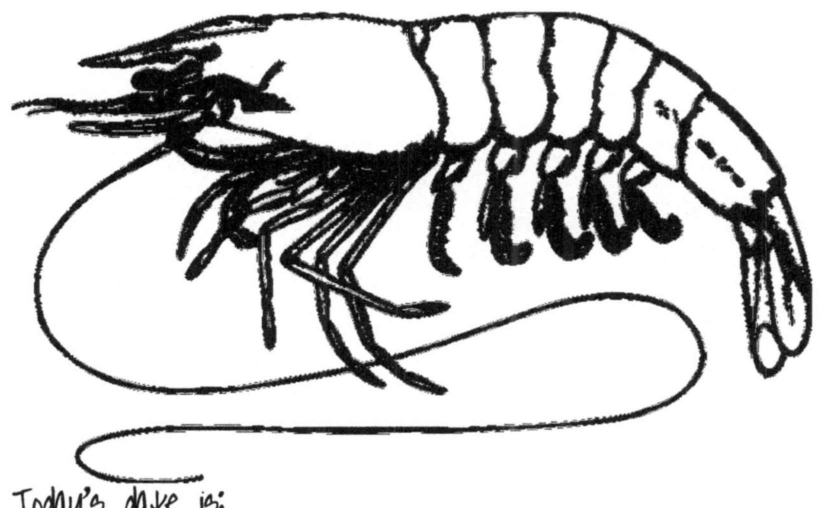

Today's date is:

____

If I get crabby or feel shrimpy this makes me happy:

All I ask is to be near the part of the earth that nestles up to water. A.K. Smith

sketch a memory.

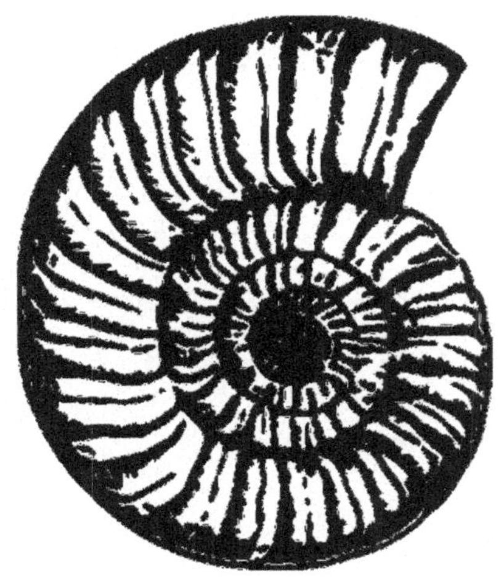

Today's date is:

____

I want to remember this about today:

The Sea of Cortez is a collection of diamonds on the water. A.K. Smith

sketch a memory:

Today's date is:

____

I want to remember my first memory of the ocean:

____

____

____

____

____

____

____

____

____

____

____

____

____

sketch a memory.

The sea is only the embodiment of a supernatural and wonderful existence-

Jules Verne

sketch a memory.

Today's date is:

____

I want to remember this about my life:

____
____
____
____
____
____
____
____
____

sketch a memory:

My big fish must be somewhere.

-Ernest Hemingway, The Old Man and the Sea

sketch a memory:

Today's date is:
I want to remember:

sketch a memory:

Thought is the wind, knowledge the sail, and mankind the vessel. – August Hare

sketch a memory:

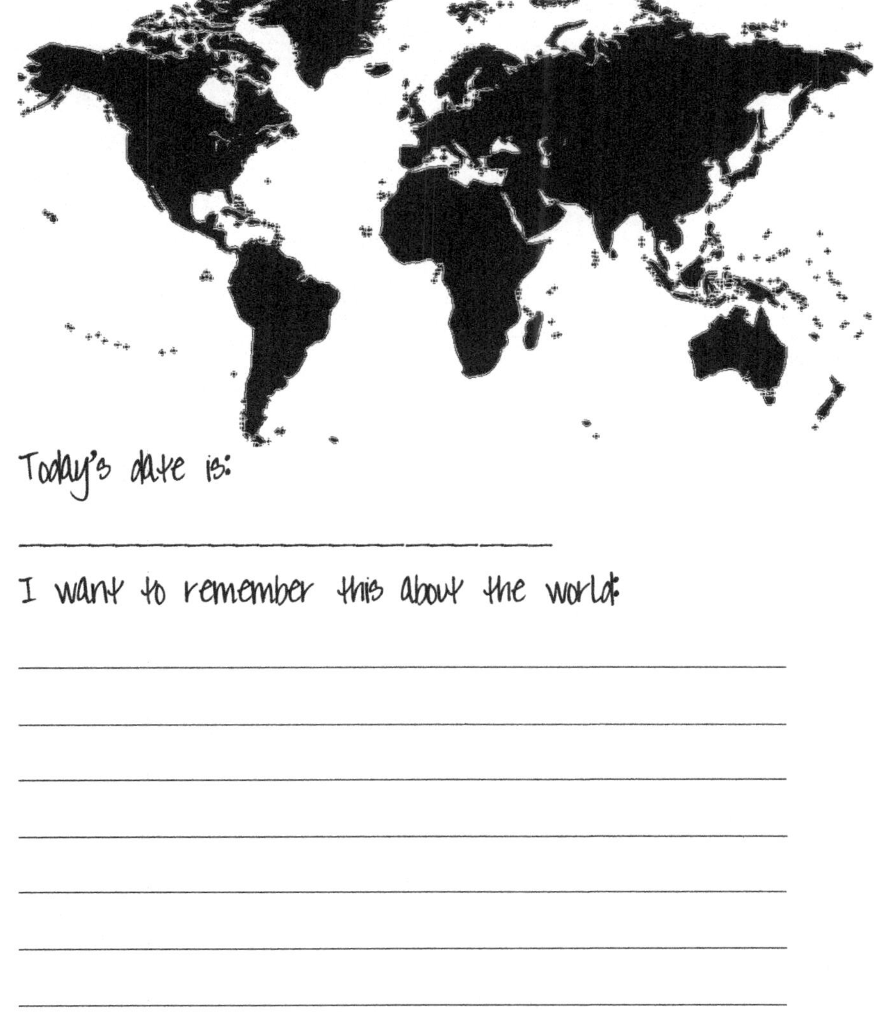

Today's date is:

____

I want to remember this about the world:

____

____

____

____

____

____

____

____

____

____

____

____

sketch a memory.

I love Van Morrison for telling me to let my soul and spirit fly. When I'm at the sea, my soul is flying in Puerto Penasco.

A.K. Smith

sketch a memory.

Today's date is:

____

I want to remember this about love:

____

____

____

____

____

____

____

____

____

sketch a memory:

I'm not afraid of storms, for I'm learning how to sail my ship.

- Louisa May Alcott

Today's date is:

____

I want to remember:

____

____

____

____

____

____

____

____

____

There might be sharks in the sea, but there are worse sharks on the land. I'll jump in.

A.K. Smith

Today's date is:

____

I hope I never forget this about vacations:

____

____

____

____

____

____

____

____

____

____

____

____

sketch a memory:

Anyone can hold the helm when the sea is calm. Publilius Syrus

Today's date is:

____

I want to remember this about the beach and flipflops:

____

____

____

____

____

____

____

____

____

____

I fear the man who drinks water and so remembers this morning what the rest of us said last night. Benjamin Franklin

Today's date is:

____

I want to remember this about today:

I'm not worried about the waves,

catching one or being caught by one.

Just as long as I can watch them roll

in. A.K. Smith

sketch a memory.

Today's date is:

____

I want to remember all the sea creatures in the Sea of Cortez:

____

____

____

____

____

____

____

____

____

____

____

____

____

Let the waves hit your feet, and the sand be your seat. Unknown

sketch a memory.

Today's date is:

____

I want to remember this about my life:

sketch a memory:

I love the people who travel to the edge of the sea, they are the ones who will never give up.

A.K. Smith

Today's date is:

____

I want to remember this about today:

sketch a memory.

Focus more on your desire than your doubt, and the dream will take care of itself. Mark Twain

Today's date is:

____

I want to remember this one Rocky Point night:

____

____

____

____

____

____

____

____

____

Happiness is when what you think, what you say, and what you do are in harmony. Gandhi

Today's date is:

____

I want to remember this about beach vacations:

____

____

____

____

____

____

____

____

____

____

____

____

You see things and you say, why? . But I dream things and I say, ' Why not?

George Bernard Shaw

Let's go to the beach? Why not?

sketch a memory:

Today's date is:

____

I want to remember what makes me happy:

The sea lives in every one of us. - *Wyland*

Thanks for taking the time to write your memories of the sea and the beautiful beaches of Puerto Penasco, aka Rocky Point, Mexico.

Keep this journal somewhere safe. If you enjoyed this book buy one for a friend or family member and pay it forward.

START A YEARLY COLLECTION.

OR

GIFT ONE AS A SPECIAL GIFT

A VARIETY OF JOURNALS EXIST: TRY ONE WITH DAILY INSPIRATIONAL QUOTES, OR WRITING PROMPTS TO KEEP YOU WRITING.

DO YOU HAVE A TRAVEL BUCKET LIST?

CHECK OUT:
TRAVEL JOURNAL:
MY TRAVEL BUCKET LIST
AND
OUR TRAVEL BUCKET LIST
BY ANITA KALTENBAUGH
ON AMAZON

Books With Soul

Books with Soul believes in sharing gifts that inspire and motivate others to create memories and keep a record of the story of their life.

WE believe every life is worth a few written words to pass on or reflect on in the future.
You don't have to be an author to tell the story of your life. Just be you.
Today will be the good old days someday, remember them.
Thank you for becoming a Memory Collector.

Questions? Email info@bookswithsoul.com
We appreciate every reader, every traveler and recorder of history.
We would love if you took the time to write a review on Amazon and let us know if the books motivated you.

Find more journals, inspiration, diaries, coloring books and gifts for every milestone at
www.bookswithsoul.com

If you would like to have a personalized journal for an organization, company, group, club, family or activity, contact Books with Soul.
Special unique journals in 20 quantities or more can be created.

*if someone bought you this journal, pay it forward and **buy a journal** for someone you care about.
Help them write the story of their life.

Other Books With Soul Journals:
Words I Want to Say
Every Breath- A Journal of Gratitude & Blessings
Crazy Ramblings of a Pregnant Woman
Remember When: Guest Book
Camp Memories
Reflections from the Beach
Reflections from Rocky Point
Pregnancy Journal: When We Were One
The Adventures of US
Reflections of My Year
Seriously I'm 50?
Old Soul

Anniversary editions available on Amazon:
1st Anniversary: One Epic Year
5th Anniversary: Five Epic Years
10th Anniversary: Ten Epic Years
15th Anniversary: Fifteen Epic Years
20th Anniversary: Twenty Epic Years
25th Anniversary: Twenty-five Epic Years
30th Anniversary: Thirty Epic Years
35th Anniversary: Thirty-five Epic Years
40th Anniversary: Forty Epic Years
45th Anniversary: Forty-five Epic Years
50th Anniversary: Fifty Epic Years

Perfect Anniversary Gift

Books with Soul ™

was inspired from a lover of music and life, who believed in the soul.

He had a collection of wonderful things. Physical memcries you could

read, touch, and listen to- including thousands of vinyl albums.

Old school music, that lasts forever. In 2018, he passed away from brain cancer, but his memory lives on as others go old school. Collect pieces

of your history, put pencil to paper, and record written memories.

A physical book will not be lost in the cloud, and will last longer than a lifetime.

Keep a record of the story of your life. Your Words. Your Pages.

This is for you Mark.

LOVE

Rocky Point

Made in the USA
Las Vegas, NV
16 December 2022

62909650R00144